TRAMS, BUSES & TROLLEYBUSES
Past and Present

No 1 LONDON

TRAMS, BUSES & TROLLEYBUSES
Past and Present
No 1 LONDON

Michael H. C. Baker

Past & Present Publishing Ltd

First published in 2010

British Library Cataloguing in Publication Data

A catalogue record for this book is available
from the British Library.

ISBN 1 85895 266 6

Past & Present Publishing Ltd
The Trundle
Ringstead Road
Great Addington
Kettering
Northants NN14 4BW

Tel/Fax: 01536 330588
email: sales@nostalgiacollection.com
Website: www.nostalgiacollection.com

Printed and bound in the Czech Republic

For Katy
In the hope that one day all London buses will be pink and purple.

**London's buses past and present: RT1797, on the 62 route in Longbridge Road, Barking,
opposite the bus garage in 1978, is contrasted with an example of London's newest single-decker,
Optare Versa 37014, also on the 62 in Longbridge Road, in June 2009.** *Both MHCB*

CONTENTS

HIGH HOLBORN: L2 Class trolleybus 1374 of Highgate Depot departs from the Charterhouse terminus of route 613 in 1960. One of the delights of driving behind a bus that is about to pull out from a stop is to let it do so and receive in gratitude the veritable Christmas-tree-like display of flashing lights that drivers now have at their disposal, although many still stick a hand out, like the driver here, and give a thumbs-up. One of the problems confronting London Transport as they replaced the trams in the 1930s was finding turning loops for the trolleybuses. The Holborn buses came down Grays Inn Road into High Holborn, turned into Charterhouse Street, then headed back along Farringdon Road towards Kings Cross and the north.

The second view shows Saunders-bodied RT1268 passing RTL2 in High Holborn in October 1955, while in 2001 an immaculate RM85 of Battersea garage heads west into the sun along High Holborn in 2001. *All MHCB*

INTRODUCTION

As long as London exists there will surely always be a need for some form of public transport. I suppose we could have begun our story back in Medieval times with kings, queens and other notables sailing up and down the Thames in their royal barges, but this would hardly have been transport for the general public. Better to begin with the many crossings of the Thames. Roads were so bad and many of the streets so dangerous that most public transport in and around London was either across or up and down the River (we are justified in using a capital letter, for to any Londoner there is only one river – the Thames).

The River lost its virtual monopoly of public transport with the advent of George Shillibeer's 22-seat omnibus in July 1829, which began to operate between the Yorkshire Stingo, a public house near St Marylebone Church, Moorgate and the Bank of England. Ever since then public houses have featured large as London bus, tram and trolleybus destinations – in my home town, Croydon (how dare you refer to it as a mere suburb!), the Red Deer, the Swan & Sugar Loaf, the Greyhound and the Black Horse instantly spring to mind. Which brings us to the geographical coverage of the volume you have in your hands. Striking a balance between central London, suburban and Home Counties locations proved the devil of an exercise and in the end, not surprisingly, the latter two suffered greatly in order to accommodate as fully as possible the former. In fact, towns served by the London Transport Country Area, which would never have considered themselves suburbs, have, reluctantly, been almost totally omitted, while coverage in detail of the vast sprawl of other towns nearer the capital, which, resist thought they might, find themselves defined as suburbia, would clearly have been quite impossible

unless the lucky reader had library shelves equal in extent to those found in one of the grander stately homes and a potential readership equal to that of the latest J. K. Rowling epic. Hopefully, the latter situation may occur once we hit the bookshops, but without a guarantee of this the publishers and I felt unable to risk all on this desirable eventuality.

So as is only right and proper that most of the settings are in the City and the West End, with a fair number further out into Kent, Surrey and Middlesex, and even into Hertfordshire and Buckinghamshire – but not much. The period covered is largely post-1945, although we go back further here and there. Thus there is a generous supply of pictures of trams, trolleybuses, motor buses and coaches, as well as a few oddities, these including a cow masquerading as a bus in the Strand, a Southdown PD2, and a coach full of Poles. The pictures reveal locations that have changed utterly, and others hardly at all. We note how knocked about London was during the Blitz and again during the 'doodlebug' and 'V2' raids of 1944-45 and how shabby it still looked ten or more years later. Buildings have generally got much taller, and much shinier, particularly in the City, and, like the people walking past them, much tidier.

As for the vehicles, there were still buses with open staircases at work in the late 1940s, an era when, like London itself, the vehicles often looked, and indeed were, neglected and worn out. The post-war RT era, in all its glorious modernity, dawned in 1947, the last pre-war buses departed in 1954, the trams having gone two years earlier (although my home town, naturally enough, brought them back, eventually), and before that decade was out the first Routemasters appeared. Ten years after the end of the London tram, its successor, the trolleybus, had also gone, despite the capital's trolleybus system once being the largest in the world. The RT and the Routemaster form a large part of our story, but huge changes began to take place even before the last RTs bowed out of ordinary public service in 1979, with declining passenger numbers and increasing traffic congestion. Much larger vehicles took over, the engine moved from beside the driver to the rear or underneath the bus – which doesn't make the bus any less 'real' – and conductors became redundant.

In 1970 the Country Area was taken from London Transport control and became part of the National Bus Company. It very soon fragmented and the evidence that it was once part of the great empire administered from 55 Broadway became increasingly hard to find. London Transport found it difficult to adapt to a changing world and its first purpose-built, high-capacity double- and single-deckers were costly failures, although this was as much due to entrenched LT attitudes as to the vehicles themselves. The great bus overhaul works at Chiswick and Aldenham became redundant as London found that it could manage quite well with more or less standard vehicles identical to those at work all over the UK.

Privatisation brought yet more upheavals, but in the end the capital was spared the chaos and uneconomic competition that deregulation wrought elsewhere. The two great manufacturers that dominated the British and London bus scene from the beginning of the 20th century, AEC and Leyland, combined, but proved unable to compete with more flexible, far-seeing and advanced foreign manufacturers. Meanwhile the familiar red London double-decker appeared to be under threat both from high-capacity single-deckers and a kaleidoscope of liveries, especially out in the suburbs.

For the enthusiast, various anniversaries, Green Line's and then London Transport's 50th, provided much enjoyment in the revival of bygone liveries; Routemasters went silver, then gold, to celebrate the Queen's 25th and 50th Jubilees, and there were many other celebratory events. The enthusiast movement grows, and the London Omnibus Traction Society provides a wealth of regular information undreamed of in earlier times, although the Ian Allan *ABC*s, the first of which came out at the end of the war, were a wonder of the age.

The London Transport Collection of vintage vehicles finally went on view at the Museum of British Transport in the former Clapham bus garage in the 1960s. Meanwhile enthusiasts themselves begin to preserve old London buses, beginning with T31 in 1956, and this movement has grown in an extraordinary manner, ranging from enthusiasts with just one vehicle, which they may or may not be able to properly restore and maintain, to an organisation such as the London Bus Preservation Trust at Cobham, which has a collection rivalling that of the official one.

After decades of decline, a variety of factors, not least increasing congestion and pollution and the introduction of systems enabling passengers to pay for bus journeys either before boarding or afterwards, has seen a steady increase in patronage. This has meant the double-decker once again becoming the norm, and legislation has ensured that it will be painted, whoever its owner, in traditional red. To travel in a beautiful big red double-decker bus in the capital today is to realise that London, while no longer the heart of an empire imposed on much of the rest of our planet, is more than ever a world city where people from all over the world have chosen to come and live either for a time or to settle permanently. As I write this, the Copenhagen Conference on global warming is struggling to find solutions for the future. One certainty is that more and more use will have to be made of public transport. So climb aboard a big London double- or indeed single-decker and you will find yourself part of that future now.

The City

TOWER BRIDGE: RTL1411 heads southbound across the bridge on route 42 in 1955.

On 12 December 2009 preserved RML1033 heads north over Tower Bridge on a Christmas Lights tour. There was once a rumour that the American who bought the old London Bridge when it was replaced in the 1960s thought he was actually getting the rather more distinctive Tower Bridge! *Both MHCB*

ALDGATE must be one of the most valuable bus station sites in the country, situated as it is within a few hundred yards of the heart of the City of London. The first picture dates from 1940: on the left is an almost new STL2612, in two-tone green livery and dating from August 1939, working Green Line service Z1, while alongside is central area STL2321 dating from October 1937 on route 42.

The second view is an early post-war picture of Tilling ST914, pressed into emergency service on the 42 at Aldgate, rather the worse for wear with a sag in its bodywork. Withdrawn around the time of the declaration of war, but not scrapped, the Tilling STs were sent to help out all over the country. Afterwards, although scrapping had begun, some reappeared on the streets of London, helping out during the shortages of the late 1940s. One, ST922, has survived, thanks to the efforts of the late Prince Marshall

ST PAUL'S: Craven-bodied RT1474 heads past the Cathedral in 1949 on its way to the route 15 terminus at Aldgate.

Below: A number of standard Routemasters used on the sightseeing tour were lengthened by having an extra bay inserted and reclassified ERM. This is ERM235 beside St Paul's in 1999.

Above: A rather different sightseeing tour is that undertaken by vintage buses each December. RT1784, ahead of RM1033, pauses outside St Paul's on 12 December 2009. *Author's collection/MHCB (2)*

LUDGATE CIRCUS: This is the view looking towards St Paul's during the First World War, with B Types prominent.

Looking down Ludgate Hill towards the Circus and Fleet Street we see Metroline TP41, a Plaxton President-bodied Dennis Trident, on route 4, while London General WVL136 on route 11, advertising an Oscar-winning film – cinema adverts have always been a feature of London buses – heads west in March 2009. *Author's collection/MHCB*

The Lord Mayor of London descends Ludgate Hill in his coach during the 1980 Lord Mayor's Show. Behind, the bomb site from 1940 had still not been built on. *MHCB*

ROYAL COURTS OF JUSTICE: In 1949, at the top of Fleet Street, where it becomes the Strand, an ST and an RT head past the boundary between the West End and the City at Temple Bar towards Ludgate Circus, with another early roof-box RT approaching.

Outside the Law Courts on 27 March 2009 is East London 18267, an ADL Trident with an ALX400 body, on route 15. *Author's collection/MHCB*

HOLBORN VIADUCT was built in the 1860s at the enormous cost of £2 million to improve access from the West End to the City of London. Newly delivered Craven-bodied RT1479 has just passed under the viaduct as it heads south along Farringdon Street on route 63, passing a 1939 Vauxhall saloon.

In March 2009 Metroline Volvo/Transbus VP499 is at the same location working route 17. *Author's collection/MHCB*

This December 2009 view from the Viaduct is looking down on a London Central Volvo/Alexander working the 63.

In 1952, just beyond the western end of Holborn Viaduct, private hire RF2 is in the foreground with an STL opposite and two trolleybuses about to turn out of High Holborn into Charterhouse Street. Immediately to the right is one of the many bomb sites that still littered the City of London.

HOLBORN in 1949 sees LT541 on the 63 and an ST on the 4A opposite.

DAF/Transbus LJ03 stands in Holborn by the Viaduct in December 2009. Behind is a fine example of the mix of 19th, 20th and 21st century architecture that is such a feature of central London. So pleased, justifiably, were the Victorians with Holborn Viaduct and the improvement in traffic flow – all of it, of course, horse-powered – that they erected four larger-than-life allegorical figures on the Viaduct, one of which can be seen on the extreme right. *Author's collection/Pamlin/ MHCB*

The West End

ALDWYCH: Looking west from Fleet Street in 1998 we see St Mary-le-Strand church in the heart of the Aldwych with, in the foreground, preserved 'sit up and beg' STL469 on its way to Covent Garden.

On the opposite side of the road, looking east on 18 May 2004, a London General Volvo B7TL with Wright Eclipse Gemini bodywork and overall advertising for a West End show is about to pass from the West End to the City of London. *Both MHCB*

ALDWYCH: Looking westwards from the other end of Aldwych towards Trafalgar Square, in 1972, among the traffic are, from left to right, a Red Arrow Merlin (just coming into the picture), an RM, another Merlin, an RT and RM971, in all-over advertising livery for Yellow Pages.

Looking in the opposite direction in May 2009 we see, from left to right, RM1933, in a special livery of deep maroon and silver to mark the centenary of Bow Garage; a London United Volvo B7TL with an East Lancs Omnidekka body on route 9; PVL53, a London Central Volvo BNTL with a Plaxton President body; and an RM on route 9. *Both MHCB*

Six months later, and the upper, northern, side of Aldwych looking east, we see RM1933 again, but now it has been repainted in 1933 London Transport livery. It is standing alongside a London General Volvo/Wrightbus advertising the long-running West End show The Lion King. *MHCB*

Two environmentally friendly modes of transport cross from Waterloo Bridge into Aldwych in 2005. Alongside the cyclist is one of the unique 'steam' buses, an experimental fuel-cell-powered Mercedes-Benz Citaro, on route RV1. This was one of many examples of attempts to combat climate change and provide non-polluting city buses. *MHCB*

On display at the Strand end of the Aldwych in July 2002 is this delightful cow doing its best to look like a bus. It was one of a number of decorated sculptured cows displayed around London streets. *MHCB*

STRAND: RTW1 is working route 8 eastbound in the Strand in 1958.

A great surprise in the spring of 1993 was the appearance of 24 Routemasters in the attractive livery of Kentish Bus when that company was awarded the route 19 contract. RML 2574 in seen in the Strand.

Equally attractive was the livery applied to the London & Country Volvos, which took over route 176 in November 1996. H674 GPF was also photographed in the Strand. *All MHCB*

TRAFALGAR SQUARE: One could fill a book with pictures taken in what many would consider the heart of the capital, Trafalgar Square, but we will have to settle for this selection. At some time in the late 1920s a Tilling Stevens TS3A petrol-electric open-topper, XH 9289, which would not have looked out of place a couple of decades earlier, emerges from the Strand and seems to be only just avoiding the water hydrant as it enters the square.

Waiting at the lights to enter Trafalgar Square on 24 March 1959 are RTL1318 and RTs 2768 and 473.

In the third view, one of the first production post-war RTs and an ST pass the South African Embassy in 1948.

Finally, at the same location but photographed from across the road in the square is RM623, with beyond it RM1933, which has become very much a celebrity bus and can still be seen regularly working around Trafalgar Square. It first appeared in the attractive 1933 replica livery to celebrate London Transport's 50th anniversary in 1983 and is seen in that year. *Author's collection/ MHCB/Author's collection/MHCB*

TRAFALGAR SQUARE: In this 1941 picture, taken outside Charing Cross station looking towards the square, are an ST on route 15 and a Hendon STD. Given the date, it is hardly surprising that there are so many uniforms in evidence.

In December, 2004 two RMLs are seen at the same location, highlighted by the low midday winter sun.
Author's collection/MHCB

TRAFALGAR SQUARE: The very last Routemaster, RML2760, worked for a time on the East London express commuter X15 from March 1989, and is seen here in that year at its terminus ahead of one of the former British European Airways front-entrance Routemasters that also worked the X15.

The 159 was the very last ordinary Routemaster route. Seen from a following Volvo, (with sun visor strip) the penultimate member of the class, RML2759, is about to enter the Square from Whitehall in 2004.

On 8 December 2005 extraordinary scenes stopped the public in their tracks and brought photographers out by the hundred to mark the penultimate day of ordinary Routemaster operation in London. One of the many surprises to turn up on route 159 was preserved Hants & Dorset ECW-bodied K6A HLJ 44, which was delivered new in 1949 to help out London's chronic shortage of buses, before being sent to its rightful owners. *All MHCB*

TRAFALGAR SQUARE: For a while in the early 1970s Prince Marshall's preserved Tilling ST922 worked tourist bus service No 100 and is seen here in 1972 on the south side of the Square.

A Brixton RML at dusk in February 2004, with some of the crowds that always flock, like the now banished pigeons, around the Square.

Several buses carried an overall 'Back the Bid' livery for the 2012 Olympics, although it cannot be proved that they accounted for its success. One such was Metroline 535, LK04 CUJ, a Transbus President-bodied Volvo B7TL. *All MHCB*

VICTORIA EMBANKMENT:
Left: The Embankment was sheer heaven for lovers of London trams and they continued to serve it until the very last day of tram operation, on 5 July 1952. Shortly before that date we see two E3s, Nos 1940 and 1979.

In about 1937, as an HR2 heads eastwards, a 1930-vintage Green Line T Class Regal approaches, and among the other traffic are three private-hire coaches parked on the left of the picture.

Although new RTs and RTLs were mostly used to replace the trams, a surprise at the very end of the replacement programme was the appearance of some pre-war STLs and 2RT2s. STL822 stands on the now redundant tracks ahead of RTL29 later that July. *Author's collection (2)/D. A. Jones*

VICTORIA EMBANKMENT: Gradually the replacement bus services quit the Embankment for Whitehall and other streets, which passengers found more convenient. The 109, which took over from the 18/20 trams, was one of the very few left there in 1980.

Sightseeing Alexander-bodied Olympian is seen at the same location on 27 March 2009. The notion of riding open-top along the Embankment in March would have seemed very odd to Londoners in the tram era, once the very early open-toppers had either been scrapped or upgraded, particularly in the severe winters of the 1940s. *Both MHCB*

Opposite page: PICCADILLY CIRCUS: Service and tourist buses are again contrasted in the iconic location of Piccadilly Circus in 1955 and 2009. *Both MHCB*

OXFORD STREET: Nowhere in London do buses congregate in such large numbers, possibly for mutual protection, possibly as a gift to bus-spotters. It was always thus, as demonstrated by this wonderful collection of LTs, STs, STLs seen in 1948 outside Selfridges, together with a glimpse of an STD on route 13 as well as examples of the latest fashions.

The second photograph is a January 2009 scene outside Selfridges, and the third is a view from inside preserved RT1784 on a Christmas Lights tour as it passes Selfridges, which was celebrating its centenary, on 12 December 2009. Finally, the telephoto lens reveals in this 2005 picture that Oxford Street – this section long restricted to buses and taxis – sports a surprising amount of greenery. *All MHCB*

PARK LANE: The 'Pre-war' RTs were withdrawn from passenger service in 1955, except for seven that were repainted green and worked from Hertford from 1955 to 1957, and continued to serve as trainers for a number of years after that. RT123, dating from 1940, is seen passing a street-sweeper and pursued by a rather interesting-looking sports car in 1956.

Dial-a-Ride minibus YX08 FKR speeds along Park Lane in April 2010. *Both MHCB*

HYDE PARK CORNER: In 1949 a Green Line 10T10, two STLs, an LT and an ST are seen on the north side of the traffic island.

Some Green Line services have survived into the 21st century, such as the 797 seen here in Park Lane leaving Hyde Park Corner and worked by Sovereign on 24 April 2004.

Rather like the start of a Grand Prix race is this line-up at Hyde Park Corner looking east on 15 January 2009. From left to right, they are Transdev VLE8 and heritage RM1218, both on route 9, First VNL32266 on the 10, and a 44 in the second row. *Author's collection/ MHCB (2)*

Westminster and Victoria

WHITEHALL: In 1948, looking towards Trafalgar Square, we see an LT in the foreground with an STL, an RT, a D and an ST further away.

On 3 December 2005 RM1292, its registration a reminder that it served for a while in Scotland before returning to London, advertises the fact that although the 159 and thus all regular Routemaster operation will be over in days, the heritage routes will still operate Routemasters.

Although open-top buses now operate all the year round in London, there is no guarantee of suitable weather for such enterprises even in mid-summer. In June 1992 pupils and teachers of Swanage Middle School look more than a trifle damp on the top deck of an open-top Routemaster passing the Cenotaph; another passes in the opposite direction.

Finally, preserved RT3062 heads westwards along Whitehall on 8 December 2005 ahead of a Mercedes 'bendy bus' on route 12. *Author's collection/MHCB (3)*

PARLIAMENT SQUARE: Preserved Tilling ST922 based at Cobham Bus Museum swings out of Parliament Square into Whitehall on 8 December 2005.

On 27 March 2009 Transdev Scania SP31, YN08 DHX, is seen passing the same corner. *Both MHCB*

BRIDGE STREET: LT634 stands outside Westminster Underground station in Bridge Street, between Parliament Square and Westminster Bridge, in 1948 on its way to Plumstead Common.

Transdev Scania SP131 of 2010 is outside the station on its way to another South East London destination in April 2010. *Author's collection/ MHCB*

WESTMINSTER BRIDGE: It's 10 o'clock and a virtually brand-new LCC D Class bogie car of 1904 is in the foreground with four-wheel open and closed cars beyond. The rest of the traffic appears to be entirely horse-powered.

At the same location some 25 or more years later the time by Big Ben has moved on to 20 minutes to 11, and we see E1 car No 798 of 1907, a T Type Green Line coach, an LGOC K open-top double-decker, an NS beyond that, and in the distance a brand-new LT, which puts all the other vehicles, other than the coach, to shame with its modernity.

Finally, it is 2.40pm on 8 December 2005, and preserved RMC1453 is working the 159. *Author's collection/Pamlin/MHCB*

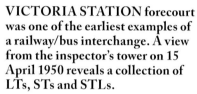

VICTORIA STATION forecourt was one of the earliest examples of a railway/bus interchange. A view from the inspector's tower on 15 April 1950 reveals a collection of LTs, STs and STLs.

Seven years later the RT family reigns supreme: RTs 1932, 331 and 1313 are seen on 20 May 1957.

The third view is from the 'bendy bus' era, 5 November 2007, with MA94 and MA37.

Finally, Transdev Scania/East Lancashire SO2 stands at Victoria in May 2009. *All MHCB*

VAUXHALL BRIDGE ROAD: Round the corner from Victoria Coach Station was the terminus of seven weekday tram services. Rehabilitated 1398 and a Feltham are seen there in 1949.

A Metroline Dennis Trident/Plaxton President and a General Volvo/Plaxton on the tram replacement route are seen in Vauxhall Bridge Road, this section now a one-way street, in October 2008. *Author's collection/MHCB*

BUCKINGHAM PALACE ROAD: What address could be more grand than this? London's most famous route, the 11, passes Eccleston Bridge and Victoria Coach Station as it heads westwards along this thoroughfare, where a Leyland Titan TD1 of the independent Express stands in 1932, before that company was absorbed into the London Transport fleet a year later. Behind is a London General ST.

A London General Volvo B7TL with a Wright Eclipse Gemini body is at the same location in June 2009.

Finally, Green Line coach YJ58 FHZ is working the 757 Luton Airport service in February 2009. Two National Express coaches are on the opposite side of the road. *Author's collection/MHCB (2)*

VICTORIA COACH STATION is
London's principal coach station. The
splendid art deco building dates from 1932
and was the work of Thomas Wallis, who was
also responsible for the iconic Firestone and
Pyrene factories out in the western suburbs.

Although mostly used by long-distance
traffic, over the years London Transport
coaches have appeared here; in 1958 one of
the original private-hire AEC Regal Mark IV
coaches of 1951 emerges.

At the same location in 2009 one of the
frequent X90 Oxford coaches pulls out.
There was a time when Green Line buses
reached Oxford. *Postcard/MHCB (2)*

VICTORIA COACH STATION:
Double-deck buses would occasionally appear on long-distance services in the 1950s, and here Southdown Park Royal-bodied PD2 No 766 swings out into Buckingham Palace Road on its way to Worthing on a Saturday in June 1955.

Today young backpackers from all over the world are a familiar sight around Victoria. Behind a well-loaded couple is a First coach working a Green Line relief in February 2009.

Very much a phenomenon of the 21st century at Victoria are coaches from far-flung parts of Europe. Here a coach from Poland is arriving in December 2008. *All MHCB*

ECCLESTON BRIDGE, spanning Victoria railway station and across the road from the coach station, was long the principal Green Line boarding point in London. For a time in the late 1950s Gillingham Street garage (GM), a few hundred yards from the bridge, was the resting place for the fleet of Green Line RTs, which would come up from the country in the morning and depart thence in the evening. Prominent are RTs 3605, 620 and 3438.

The Green Line network is much reduced today but some services remain popular. One of the massive six-wheel Acron/Van Hool coaches sets off for Luton Airport in February 2009. *Both MHCB*

West and South West London

HAMMERSMITH: In 1936 an almost new STL on route 11 and an E1 tram on route 28 pass the Underground station. Both tram and bus will serve Victoria, but by very different routes; the Hammersmith to Wandsworth section of the tram route will soon be taken over by trolleybuses.

In the second photograph N1, F1 and Q1 trolleybuses stand at Hammersmith on 8 July, 1960.

A large amount of rebuilding has taken place in Hammersmith over the intervening years, but in this 2009 picture of the bus station the five-storey building, the George, seen in the first picture, survives, just behind the arriving trolleybus replacement 266. *London Transport Museum/MHCB (2)*

SHEPHERDS BUSH was once the haunt of highwaymen, but is quite the opposite today, its market a source of bargains. Two wartime D Class Daimlers from Merton Garage take a breather in 1949, D132 before returning on route 49 to Crystal Palace, and D153 on the 88 to Clapham Common.

On the south side on 26 November 1960 are trolleybuses 661 and 691, MCW-bodied Leylands of 1937 vintage, flanking 1875, one of the final batch of London trolleybuses, a Q1 of 1952, which when it went into service was part of the largest trolleybus fleet in the world.

At the same location on 1 December 2009 Transdev Volvo/Transbus VA299 is on trolleybus replacement 220. *Author's collection/MHCB (2)*

SLOUGH is not the prettiest of places – just ask John Betjeman – nor is it the quietest, being right under Jumbo jets taking off from or landing at the world's busiest international airport. Perhaps it might be claimed that in its rather brutalist bus station it got what it deserved. An Alder Valley Leyland National, RML2307 and RF122 are seen there in 1978.

In April 2009 a bus rally based on Slough created this splendid throwback to the 1970s with RF457 and RML2412 featured in the bus station. The station and the car park above were knocked down early in 2010: few tears were shed. *Both MHCB*

**HAMPTON COURT: L3 trolleybus
1426 swings around at the Hampton Court
terminus of the 667 in front of the gates of
Cardinal Wolsey's/Henry VIII's Palace on 25
January 1961.**

On a sunny June day in 2008 No 8069,
a Travel Surrey Transbus Dart heads over
the Thames past the roundabout seen in the
previous picture. *Both MHCB*

HAMPTON COURT: In 1977, in the forecourt of Hampton Court station, immediately beyond the bridge and on the opposite bank from the Palace, a lady waits patiently to gain admittance to RF326, no doubt a rather more reliable prospect than either of the two DMSs, the leading one being DMS1504.

In this 2005 picture at the same location the driver of a Travel London Dart/Plaxton President is about to assume command. *Both MHCB*

KINGSTON, a 45-minute walk along the river from Hampton Court, also has royal connections, if not so immediately obvious. The garage was one of the relatively few that also served as a bus station. Being close to the Surrey countryside it always operated an unusually large number of fairly low-density single-deck routes. In this 1950 picture LT1428 is loading up alongside a recently delivered RTW, while to the left are a former LGOC T and a later 10T10, a former Green Line coach.

Nine years later two of the Mann Egerton-bodied Leyland PS1 Tigers, TD127 and TD118, await their crews, who are in animated conversation on 12 May 1959.

Finally, on a wet night in 1975 RF369 wonders whether to venture out. *Author's collection/MHCB (2)*

KINGSTON: The garage has now gone, but today Kingston has no fewer than two bus stations. Trolleybuses served Kingston until the very end of the London trolleybus system in 1962. No 1781, one of the 1948 Q1s, the finest of them all, heads over Kingston Bridge on 12 March 1959. Pleasant though the Thames-side area might be, these vehicles were about to take themselves off to altogether hotter surroundings in Spain.

Brand-new Transdev SP52, a Scania N230UD Omnicity not yet in passenger service, heads over the bridge on 11 August 2009. *Both MHCB*

PUTNEY COMMON: RTW276 arrives at the terminus of route 22 in 1962, while in February 2010, nearly 50 years later, the preserved RT1 recreates what was once an everyday scene when 'Pre-war' RTs worked the 22. *Both MHCB*

WIMBLEDON: RT1692, sporting the GB plates it acquired when sent to Northern Europe in 1951 to publicise the Festival of Britain, stands alongside Wimbledon Common on 20 May 1957.

DOE23, a new AD Trident/Optare Olympus, is on the 93 route at the same location in March 2009 – and not a Womble in sight in either picture! *Both MHCB*

WIMBLEDON tram terminus is host to E1 1837 on route 4 (left) and E3 1877, an unusual visitor on a special working in 1950.

A few yards from the same location in the summer of 2008, Volvo/East Lancs EVL51 is nearest the camera. *Pamlin/MHCB*

MORDEN: Charles Holden is only now being recognised as one of the greatest architects of the 20th century, his work for the Underground Group and London Transport, from the headquarters at 55 Broadway to a wonderful range of stations, being much celebrated today. Morden, seen here in June 1927, was his first Tube station to be completed. Just two buses, a double-deck S and a single-deck ADC, occupy the forecourt.

The arrival of the Tube brought vast changes and the building of thousands of dwellings in what had until then been rural Surrey. In this picture, taken in 1952, D4, a lowbridge Daimler working the 127, poses beside the station entrance. Every one of the 281 wartime and early post-war D Class could be seen at Morden at some time or other, which became known to us bus-spotters as 'Daimlerland'.

By April 2008 an upper storey had been added to the station and parade of shops, and the 118 is now worked by London General. *Pamlin/Author's collection/MHCB*

63

South and South East London

LONDON BRIDGE STATION: Much damaged during the Second World War, the bus terminus at London Bridge was eventually properly reorganised in the station forecourt and a roof fitted. In this October 1979 picture RML2710 and a DMS await the off.

This is the same location on 21 November 2009 but looking in the opposite direction, with an Arriva Mercedes MA105 on route 149. *Both MHCB*

SOUTHWARK: In the evening shadows two Red Arrow Merlins and a DMS stand in a side street in April 1978 with Southwark Cathedral dominating the background.

At the same location on 1 December 2009 the low winter sun picks out the Cathedral while Metroline TPL on the 43 pursues a 141. *Both MHCB*

ELEPHANT & CASTLE has been very nearly the busiest of all London crossroads since the days of the horse. A number of LGOC B Type buses and an assortment of LCC four-wheel and bogie tramcars prove the point in 1920.

Thirty years later 2167, the only experimental prototype Feltham tram to survive into post-war years, is heading for Blackfriars Bridge and the Embankment. Ahead of it is a Tilling STL from Croydon (TC) garage on route 133 bound for Liverpool Street. The corner public house is now advertising Watneys Ales rather than Claymore whisky – is this an indication of the changing tastes of the locals? To the right is evidence of the terrible bombing that rained down on this inner London suburb during the Blitz. *The Elephant Never Forgets* was the title of a delightful official film made to commemorate the end of the first generation of London trams in 1952.

Today Elephant & Castle has changed out of all recognition, and has even acquired some greenery. It is, however, as busy as ever. In this September 2008 picture a Go Ahead Volvo/Wright WVL is heading for Streatham on the 133, while further back is a 'bendy bus' on route 12. Once both these routes served Croydon, but increasing traffic congestion has meant that they have been cut back from the outer suburbs. *London Transport Collection/V. K. C. Jones/MHCB*

BLACKFRIARS ROAD: In about 1948 we see a remarkably varied collection of London Transport trams, including E1s, E3s and a Feltham, and STL buses heading south.

Every December a number of preserved London buses and coaches take part in a tour of central London, in particular its Christmas illuminations. Taking a rest on Blackfriars Road on 12 December 2009 is RT1784 being overtaken by brand-new LX59 CYE on route 63. *Author's collection/MHCB*

LAMBETH BRIDGE: A not overcrowded STL436 on the 77 crosses the bridge on its way south in 1951. With most of its windows open it is obviously a warm day.

The final RTs and RTLs were delivered in 1954, but London Transport had overestimated its needs and a number were put into store. One such was RTL1610. It did not enter service until late 1958 and is seen here on the 77A on 21 March 1959, still in pristine, advert-less condition heading south over Lambeth Bridge.

London Transport's first real coaches were the 15 RFWs of 1951, fitted with ECW 39-seat bodies mounted on AEC Regal Mark IV chassis. In the third picture, dating from 1952, RFW7 is crossing Lambeth Bridge, with RT2384 following.

The last picture is the view from a 'bendy bus' crossing the bridge in May 2009, with a sightseeing six-wheeler – shades of the LTs – brought back from Hong Kong, approaching. It was around this time I had an argument with a Deputy Mayor of London who was pouring scorn on 'bendy buses', or to be precise the Mercedes-Benz Citaros. I pointed out that, much as I liked Routemasters, it was vastly easier to wheel my two-year-old grandson, Ben, into a 'bendy bus'. His reply was a snort. The expenses scandal did for him shortly afterwards.
MHCB (2)/Pamlin/MHCB

VAUXHALL: The fact that the tram was environmentally an ideal vehicle for carrying large numbers of people around towns and cities could not save its extinction in London in 1952. Sadly, plans to bring it back, other than the Croydon Tramlink network, have stalled, although elsewhere in the UK and abroad it has become the height of fashion. The next best thing perhaps is this diesel-electric hybrid Wright Group bus, working the 360 at Vauxhall in March 2009

A series of bridges carry Vauxhall station and the main South Western line into Waterloo over the complicated road network where routes from Brixton, Stockwell, Wandsworth and elsewhere converge beside the Thames. E3 tram 1908 is on an enthusiasts' tour in 1951.
MHCB/ Author's collection

CLAPHAM COMMON: RML2674, on the 137, heads down Long Road, alongside Clapham Common, in November 2001.

On 26 January 2009 VDL/Wrightbus DW80 is seen at the same location. *Both MHCB*

STOCKWELL: This is the crossroads where South Lambeth Road, Clapham Road and Stockwell Road meet, seen in the 1920s. LCC E Class tram 436 on route 8 is heading for Tooting, while a London General NS heads for Clapham Common.

In February 2009 London General PVL374 is seen at the same location on tram replacement route 155. *Pamlin/MHCB*

STOCKWELL GARAGE: Few bus garages could ever claim to be architectural gems, but Stockwell, completed in 1953, is the exception, being a fine example of adventurous architecture – although more by accident than design. Because of a shortage of steel, reinforced concrete had to be used and the result was the series of sweeping arches seen in this picture taken in 1970, with RTs and RMs parked outside.

In February 2009 an Alexander Dennis BAE hybrid system 'green' bus is being checked at the garage prior to taking up work on route 16. *Both MHCB*

STOCKWELL GARAGE: In 1979 RM2171, repainted in a striking red and yellow livery for the short-lived Shoplinker service, has just passed through the washing bay.

Stockwell Garage had surplus capacity for many years, hence the Scottish coaches, parked here before returning on the overnight services to Glasgow and Edinburgh, in the company of RML2724, a Leyland emergency vehicle based on a PD3 bus chassis, and two former Bournemouth double-decker Daimlers used as sightseeing vehicles. *Both MHCB*

BRIXTON has long been one of the most cosmopolitan areas of London. This view from in front of the Town Hall, officially Lambeth Town Hall, is looking north in 1951, with RT2533 on tram replacement route 195 alongside E3 tram 1995, with more RTs in the distance.

Each year on the first Sunday in May the Historic Commercial Vehicle Club stages its London to Brighton run. It begins at Crystal Palace and on the extremely wet 2 May 2010 an AEC Mammoth eight-wheel lorry dating from 1952 and bearing the British Road Services logo on its cab door precedes Arriva DLA166 on the 249 at the top of Anerley Hill. *Author's collection/MHCB*

CRYSTAL PALACE: For a while in the late 1960s preserved buses were stored in the goods yard at Crystal Palace Low Level station. The only surviving complete London 'wartime' bus, John Lines G351, is seen in 1968. It is now at the Cobham Bus Museum.

The yard has long been a residential area, as seen in the November 2009 photograph. *Both MHCB*

A night time view in the Parade in 1976, with an MD ahead of RMs and RTs. *MHCB*

The area around Crystal Palace has long supported various sporting venues and activities. Here a group of cyclists meet on a sharp, sunny January morning in 2007 with a Travel London Trident turning behind them. *MHCB*

GREENWICH: Titan T832 is at the terminus of route 108B in 1990, in a picture taken from the corner of the grounds of the National Maritime Museum. I once saw Millvina Dean, the last living survivor of the sinking of the *Titanic*, at a lecture there. The masts of the tea clipper *Cutty Sark*, which at the time of the next 'past' picture was still afloat and anchored in a rather sad state further down river alongside the training ship HMS *Worcester*, but was by 1990 preserved in dry dock, are just visible.

GREENWICH: Travel London VolvoBT7L/Wrightbus Gemini is seen at the same location in June 2009. Sadly the masts of the *Cutty Sark* have disappeared after a disastrous fire, but restoration was under way. *Both MHCB*

GREENWICH, home of the Royal Observatory, the Meridian line and the National Maritime Museum, would be deeply insulted if referred to as 'merely' a London suburb. In this April 1951 picture an E3 tram is emerging from Nelson Road on route 58, with E1 840 on route 68.

At the same location in the summer of 2009 is Enviro 400 9430. The buildings themselves remain the same but have been vastly smartened up since the austere years of the very early 1950s, when the suburbs of London were still recovering from the effects of the war.
Pamlin/MHCB

BLACKHEATH: I always associate the wide open spaces of Blackheath with Dickens's *A Tale of Two Cities* and the messenger from Tellson's Bank catching the mail coach here as it toiled up the steep hill on its way to Dover. Probably nothing so dramatic would have prompted the passengers to climb aboard this Catford (TL) RT, crossing the Heath in 1974. *(below)*

One of the handsome but short-lived Metro-Scania MDs *(above)*, which nevertheless played an important part in the development of the London bus, speeds eastwards across the Heath in 1977.

Thirty years later, on 3 February 2007, a London Central PVL was photographed at the same location on the Heath. *All MHCB*

WOOLWICH has long been of great military and naval importance, situated as it is on the south bank of the Thames within easy access of both the open sea and the centre of the capital. The establishment of the Arsenal confirmed its status and, incidentally, was where one of London's most successful football teams had its origins. In Edwardian times two E Class trams of the London County Council work their way through crowded Beresford Square in front of the main entrance to the Arsenal.

The London tram was meant to be swept away by the trolleybus, but the outbreak of the Second World War put an end to this notion, so for some 17 years Woolwich was one of the places where trams and trolleybuses met. In the summer of 1951 an E3 tram eases round the corner as it pulls away, with the Arsenal in the background, in front of which is a trolleybus. Alongside the public house is a rather weary looking Hillman van.

BARKING: The most surprising participant in the final RT parade on 7 April 1979 was none other than RT1, its restoration only completed that morning. Here it prepares to head the parade watched by excited spectators. Many of the locals, particularly those whose flats, directly opposite the bus garage, were constantly being invaded, took the enthusiasts to be barking mad (sorry!).

A rather less animated spectator waits to take over at the same location in June 2009. *Both MHCB*

BARKING GARAGE: RT624 prepares to take part in the final parade on 7 April 1979.

Not surprisingly, the bus has been preserved and is seen here in Whitehall at dusk alongside ST922 on 8 December 2005.

In the present-day view of Barking Garage, taken in June 2009, a Dart is prominent. *All MHCB*

ILFORD town centre is seen in January 1995, with a Stagecoach East London DAF Optare Delta on the 150. Ilford, like so many of the Essex suburbs, became engulfed by London in the 19th century with the arrival of the Great Eastern Railway.

The same location in July 2009 has East London Optare Versa No 37011 on the 396 with an East London Enviro 400 behind. *Both MHCB*

North London

KING'S CROSS: 'Pre-war' RT62 in green livery is in use as a trainer in King's Cross Road outside the main-line terminus in July 1960.

The September 1999 view from St Pancras station looking across to the same location features a fine selection of buses, including an all-over advert on the back of the 91. *Both MHCB*

PANCRAS ROAD: Park Royal-bodied AEC trolleybus 1652 heads down Pancras Road between St Pancras (left) and King's Cross stations in July 1955. In the distance can be seen the gas holders, still there and very famous, for they have appeared in countless films.

On a damp day in 2009 at the same location as seen on the previous page, Dennis Dart/Plaxton Pointer DLD167 is starring. Beyond is the new entrance to St Pancras International, and opposite is the King's Cross Hotel, once threatened but now being restored. The area has always had a mixed reputation, a refuge for unfortunates and those living on the wrong side of the law, but also home to some of the finest 19th-century architecture, of which the rejuvenated St Pancras station can probably lay claim to be the very best there is. *Both MHCB*

MARYLEBONE ROAD/BAKER STREET: Further west along Marylebone Road, Green Line 10T10 T471 of Amersham Garage is heading north on the 710 past Baker Street station in 1950.

Some 60 years later two 27s and a 205 call outside the station on 1 December 2009. *Both MHCB*

These Newcastle United fans, up for the Cup, are in Marylebone Road on their way to Wembley from Baker Street station on 16 May 1998. Newcastle lost 2-0 to Arsenal, who completed the Double. RML2582 of Sovereign is about to cross Marylebone Road on its way from Golders Green to London Bridge on route 13. *MHCB*

MARYLEBONE ROAD: Not an everyday sight turning out of Hampstead Road into Marylebone Road, but on 1 September 2007, during the refurbishment of the London Transport Museum at Covent Garden, a number of the exhibits were on the move.

B340, then 94 years old, leads the procession followed by TF77, RT4712 and DMS1.

More usual fare at this location is this Metroline Volvo/Plaxton working the 134 on 1 December 2009. *Both MHCB*

HOLLOWAY ROAD: Perhaps London's most famous and busiest trolleybus junction was at the Nags Head, Holloway. P1 No 1715, the final design of pre-war trolleybus, turns out of Holloway Road on its way to Waltham Cross on 9 November 1960. A Fordson van, a Ford Consul, a Mini and an RT play lesser roles.

Heading along Holloway Road towards Holborn on the same day is L3 No 1380, the only trolleybus with an FXF registration, together with an Austin A40, an Austin A35 and a Wolsley 1500. On the opposite side of the road is the Gaumont, one of the most magnificent of all the great art deco cinemas of the inter-war years.

HOLLOWAY ROAD: London Northern Metrobus M1163 is passing what had become by 1994 the Odeon. Fortunately it is still with us and much cherished. *All MHCB*

London Suburban 208, a Northern Counties-bodied Volvo with a Liverpool registration, is seen at the Nags Head in 1994.

At the junction on 1 May 2010 an Arriva VLW is entering the picture from the left while Metroline Enviro 400 TE924 is bound for Waterloo. *Both MHCB*

GOLDERS GREEN, a part of London for long a Jewish enclave, has been a terminus and important stop not only for buses, but also for the Underground, for trams, then trolleybuses, for Green Line, for-long distance coaches and, most likely, before any of those, for highwaymen. There are few signs of the latter by 1932, when prototype Feltham No 320 is seen in MET livery.

At the same location in the spring of 2009 is Metroline Transbus Trident/President TPL293. *London Transport Museum/MHCB*

GOLDERS GREEN is seen again in 1938, with T48 nearest the camera, standing next to a single-deck LT, while beyond are two STLs, an STD and a double-deck LT.

The second photograph was taken in the spring of 1940. The Blitz has not yet begun, but preparations for what everyone knows is coming are in hand, and sandbags are prominent. A Green Line 10T10 is crossing Finchley Road, there are two STLs, under the bridge are a couple of trolleybuses, an ex-London General Central Area T is to the right of the clock tower, and a Northern Line train of 1938 Tube stock is above it all.

In the station forecourt on 26 November 1960 are RTs 2833, 2958, 3644 and 4310.

At the same location in the spring of 1995 are four RMs working routes 139 and 13 and DW35, a Dennis Dart with Wright body, which, appropriately in view of where the body was built, has a Northern Irish registration.

There has always been plenty of business for single-deckers in the Golders Green area, and in the final picture, from 1 May 2010, two Arriva Solos, which serve some of the most desirable residences in the UK in Hampstead Garden Suburb, stand ready. *London Transport collection/London Transport Museum/MHCB (3)*

NORTH FINCHLEY: No 2264, one of the relatively modern former MET G Class cars, stands at the North Finchley terminus of route 21 shortly before trolleybuses took over. Modernised around 1930, these cars were probably rather superior to the ex-LCC E1s, but all had been withdrawn and broken up by the end of 1939.